Put Beginning Readers on the Right Track with
ALL ABOARD READING™

The All Aboard Reading series is especially designed for beginning readers. Written by noted authors and illustrated in full color, these are books that children really want to read—books to excite their imagination, expand their interests, make them laugh, and support their feelings. With fiction and nonfiction stories that are high interest and curriculum-related, All Aboard Reading books offer something for every young reader. And with four different reading levels, the All Aboard Reading series lets you choose which books are most appropriate for your children and their growing abilities.

Picture Readers
Picture Readers have super-simple texts, with many nouns appearing as rebus pictures. At the end of each book are 24 flash cards—on one side is a rebus picture; on the other side is the written-out word.

Station Stop 1
Station Stop 1 books are best for children who have just begun to read. Simple words and big type make these early reading experiences more comfortable. Picture clues help children to figure out the words on the page. Lots of repetition throughout the text helps children to predict the next word or phrase—an essential step in developing word recognition.

Station Stop 2
Station Stop 2 books are written specifically for children who are reading with help. Short sentences make it easier for early readers to understand what they are reading. Simple plots and simple dialogue help children with reading comprehension.

Station Stop 3
Station Stop 3 books are perfect for children who are reading alone. With longer text and harder words, these books appeal to children who have mastered basic reading skills. More complex stories captivate children who are ready for more challenging books.

In addition to All Aboard Reading books, look for All Aboard Math Readers™ (fiction stories that teach math concepts children are learning in school) and All Aboard Science Readers™ (nonfiction books that explore the most fascinating science topics in age-appropriate language).

All Aboard for happy reading!

For Hiro Savage Kimura, cool colt—P.P.
For Sophie Margaret Sheehan—M.B.
To William, Nicole, and a special thanks
to Stefanie Z.—L.B.

Library of Congress Cataloging-in-Publication Data is available.

ISBN 0-448-42524-6 (pbk)   A B C D E F G H I J
ISBN 0-448-43230-7 (GB)   A B C D E F G H I J

Ponies

By Pam Pollack and Meg Belviso
Illustrated by Lisa Bonforte

Grosset & Dunlap • New York

What's that on the hill?

It looks like a herd of baby horses.

But it is not.

It is a herd of ponies.

A pony looks like a horse.

But it is shorter.

That is what makes

a pony a pony.

A pony is never more

than 57 inches tall.

These ponies live on a farm.

The herd is like a family.

The head of the family is the stallion.

The stallion protects

the other ponies.

They all work together.

The ponies in the herd
"talk" to each other.
One pony nickers.
That's how the ponies
greet one another.

The other pony blows

through his nose.

That shows he is happy.

A third pony flicks her tail.

What does that mean?

Nothing.

She is shooing away a fly.

Two ponies stand head to tail.

They pull their lips back.

They scratch each other's necks
with their teeth.

They are making friends.

A spotted pony stands apart.

Do you see how his ears are pointed?

He is listening for something.

Ponies can hear things people cannot.

A girl walks through the grass.

She is the pony's owner.

He is very happy to see her.

The pony runs to the fence.

He puts his nose out to be petted.

They go out riding.

She tells him where to go.

And she tells him how

fast to go.

They start out

walking.

Then they go faster.

They trot.

Walking and trotting

are called "gaits."

Cantering is a faster
gait than trotting.

Galloping is the fastest of all.
A pony can gallop
30 miles per hour.
People need
a car to go that fast.
The girl leans foward.
She holds on tight.

Back on the farm,

the girl brings the pony

to his stall.

Caring for a pony is hard work.

Besides exercise,
a pony needs
lots of
fresh water
and hay.

He needs to be
brushed and
groomed.

His stall needs
to be cleaned.

Ponies get lonely by themselves.
This pony's owner spends time
with him every day.

Ponies make good friends.

They like to have fun.

Sometimes they play jokes.

This pony has unlocked his stall.

His owner thinks that

she forgot to close it.

He does it again. And again.

She laughs.

This time she knows

who did it.

One evening a baby pony is born.

A baby pony is called a foal.

His mother is called a mare.

An hour later,

he can already walk.

It is amazing.

Newborn foal

Foal at 6 months

Full-grown pony

The foal keeps close to his mother.

His mother watches out for him.

A pony is not full-grown

until it is five or six years old.

Ponies come in many colors.

They can be white, gray, brown,

red, golden or black.

Some are a mix.

This pony has a
splash of white
between its eyes.
It is called a "star."

This pony has a line
down its face.
It is called a "stripe."

An extra-wide stripe
is called a "blaze."

The white part
here is called
a "stocking."

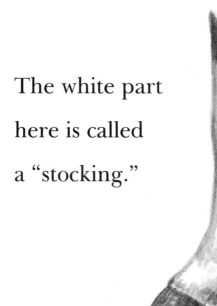

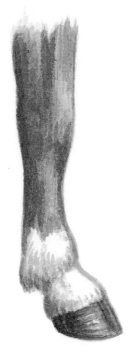

This pony's
ankle is white.
It is called a "sock."

Sable Island Pony

Highland Pony

Mustang Pony

Falabella Pony

Ponies live all over the world.

There are ponies in Europe,

Asia, and Australia.

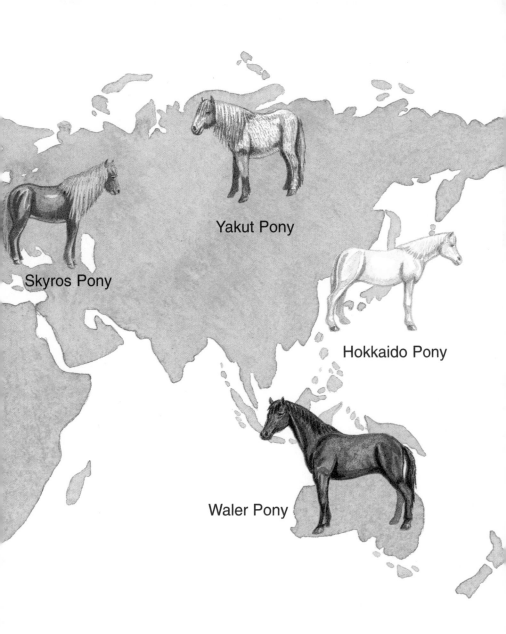

Yakut Pony

Skyros Pony

Hokkaido Pony

Waler Pony

There are ponies in
North and South America.

Most ponies live with people.

But some ponies live in the wild.

These wild ponies live

on a small island near Virginia.

The National Park Service protects them.

Once a year the ponies
are rounded up.
The ponies swim across
to another island.

It is called Chincoteague

(you say it like this: CHIN-ko-teeg).

People come from all over to watch.

A herd of wild ponies grazes in a field.

Look! A bear is nearby.

One pony snorts.

That means danger.

Another pony roars.

That means, "Look out!"

The ponies run away from the bear.

Even the foals can run very fast.

No one gets left behind.

They are all safe.

Wild ponies look out for each other.

The sun is setting.

The wild ponies rest.

And on the farm,

the girl leads her pony

back to the barn.

The girl brushes him.

She washes his face.

She cleans his hooves.

She puts a blanket over him.

She scrubs his saddle.

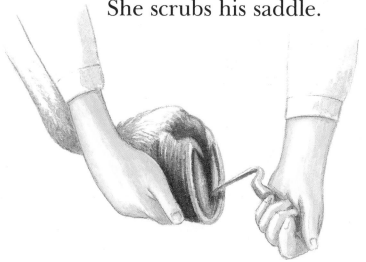

Now the pony is ready for bed.

His stall is filled with clean straw.

The straw is soft and dry.

The pony lies down.

He will have a nice deep sleep.

"Goodnight, pony," the girl says.

She closes the stall door.

The pony rubs his nose
against her cheek.
That means, "I love you."
Tomorrow he will be ready
for more fun.